CHAMPAGNE AND CAVIAR AGAIN?

Complaints of the Rich and Famous

Other Books by Joey Green and Alan Corcoran

Hellbent on Insanity
You Know You've Reached Middle Age If . . .
Senior Moments

Other Books by Joey Green

CHAMPAGNE AND CAVIAR AGAIN?

Complaints of the Rich and Famous

Joey Green, Debbie Green, *and* Alan Corcoran

Lunatic Press
Los Angeles

Published by Lunatic Press, Los Angeles
Book design by Joey Green
Distributed by Independent Publishers Group
PRINTED IN INDIA

For Barry

Visit www.lunaticpress.com

Library of Congress Control Number 2006903203

ISBN 0-9772590-0-5

10 9 8 7 6 5 4 3 2 1

Introduction

Think it's easy being rich and famous?

Quite frankly: Life on easy street is terribly bumpy.

True, nobody loves you when you're down and out, but the moment you make the Forbes 500 or win that Academy Award, the bully who broke your glasses in eighth grade is ringing your doorbell to sell you life insurance, Congress is naming a new tax bracket after you, and your gardener is suddenly closing on a second home in Aruba.

Winning the lottery may seem like the answer to all your prayers, but trust us, darling, a sudden mountain of moolah just creates an avalanche of ghastly problems. Suddenly you're forced to hire a cadre of managers, accountants, and lawyers to help you fend off the carpetbaggers, repel the paparazzi, keep the taxman at bay, and get you that coveted 2 P.M. appointment for a five-hundred-dollar haircut.

Oh, and banish the thought of spending your days simply lying around on the couch watching *Seinfeld* reruns and consuming mass quantities of Rocky Road. As the newest member of the aristocracy, it's now your civic duty to get your well-heeled derrière into the gym before it can no longer be shoehorned into a size 4. Kiss that affordable three bedroom, two-and-a-half bath in Rancho Cucamonga goodbye. Instead, say *bon jour* to your $17-million bungalow in Malibu complete with annual mudslides and brush fires.

Your old life will be a distant, sweet memory. You see, they just don't make Toyotas with bulletproof glass and fully stocked wet bars. Using a public restroom now becomes a media event. And there's really no going back once the pool guy turns out to be an ex-con who has run off with your teenage daughter and the best of your Picasso collection.

Yes, the good life definitely has a dark side. The bigger you are, the bigger the complaints. So rather than killing yourself chasing after the American Dream, kick back, pop open a bag of Oreos and a bottle of Yoo-hoo, and bask in the misery of those more fortunate than youself. Because quite honestly, it doesn't get any better than that.

Complaints of the Rich and Famous

It takes the
Pizza Hut delivery guy
thirty minutes
just to get from the
front gate of your property
to your front door.

Harvard University expects you to donate $75 million to build a new wing on the Biology Complex — every year.

Your seat on the New York Stock Exchange doesn't vibrate.

The only source for replacing your gravy boat for the good china is the Antiquities Department of the British Museum.

The wildlife preserve
you own in Kenya
declared itself
its own nation.

Daddy got you a Shetland pony for your birthday, but it was the wrong color.

The small island
you bought as a
tax write-off
turned out to be
Atlantis.

When you returned
to the restaurant
after shooting your wife,
they were out of cannoli.

You can't convince
trespassers that,
as a matter of fact,
you do own the
whole damn road.

Your hit song was featured in a commercial for Depends.

Your date refused to sign
a nondisclosure agreement
before ordering from
the menu.

YOU HAVE TO KEEP
A FRENCH TRANSLATOR
ON STAFF TO READ YOUR
SWISS BANK ACCOUNT
STATEMENTS.

Your personal chef
makes you eat all of your
Goat Cheese Stuffed Radicchio
before he'll serve
the Parmigiano-Reggiano.

*Your chauffeur
has to drive you
all the way to the lottery office
to pick up the measly
one-million-dollar prize.*

The day after
you finally dumped
your 200,000 shares
of Amazon.com stock,
the company posted
its first profit.

Jack Nicholson hurled a golf club through the windshield of your Lamborghini.

You were grateful that
the editor of your last film
digitally removed the giant zit from
your butt in all of your nude scenes—
until he won the Academy Award for
Special Effects and thanked
both the zit and your butt in
his acceptance speech.

RUDY GIULIANI SENT YOU HIS RESUME AND WON'T TAKE NO FOR AN ANSWER.

You had to apologize
to the Vice President
for getting shot
in the face.

You have
an honorary Ph.D.,
but it's from
Grenada University.

YOUR WIFE
TURNS 36 NEXT YEAR
AND YOU HAVEN'T STARTED
SHOPPING FOR A NEW ONE.

Your local liquor store doesn't carry any Scotch older than fifty years.

Your nutritionist
and your personal trainer
can't agree on
your optimal ratio of fats,
protein, and carbohydrates.

You keep getting invited to
Roseanne Arnold's
annual Christmas party
and you've run out of
believable excuses for
not being able to attend.

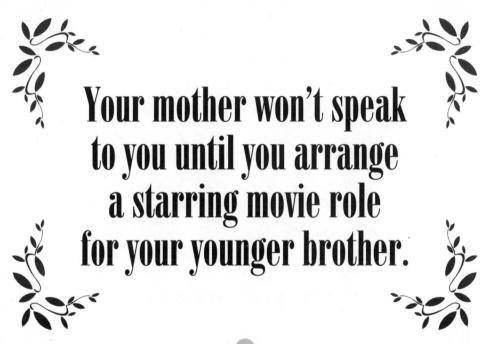

**Your mother won't speak
to you until you arrange
a starring movie role
for your younger brother.**

When you rented out Disneyland for your five-year-old son's birthday party, the Matterhorn was down for repairs.

THE DAY YOU FLEW TO
BUENOS AIRES TO PICK UP
YOUR HAND-TAILORED SHIRTS,
THEIR CURRENCY COLLAPSED.

You wish they'd stop introducing you as "and the other guy" on the Three Tenors tour.

The Queen of England won't stop asking you for real estate advice.

Singapore
refused to allow
your personal assistant
to serve a ten-year
drug sentence
in your place.

IF SHAQ LANDS IN YOUR LAP
ONE MORE TIME,
YOU'RE GIVING UP YOUR
COURTSIDE SEATS.

The wet bar
in your penthouse suite at
the Peninsula Hotel
in Hong Kong
was stocked with a
cheap plastic corkscrew.

If you fail to
tip generously at Sardi's,
your stinginess makes
Page Six of the
New York Post.

When you finally won
the Academy Award,
Jim Carrey made facial
contortions behind you
throughout your
acceptance speech.

Running the sprinklers
to keep your backyard green
during the month of August
costs more than the
gross national product
of Algeria.

When the Houston Astros play the Baltimore Orioles, you're not sure which team to root for because you own them both.

Your daughter
threw a temper tantrum
because she doesn't want the
National Security Council
screening her potential dates.

YOU HAVE FOURTEEN
DIFFERENT BRANDS OF BEER
IN THE SUB-ZERO REFRIGERATOR,
BUT THEY WON'T BE CHILLED
FOR ANOTHER 38 MINUTES.

You have to
take five Vicodin
before you can handle
singing your signature
song one more time.

Your wardrobe
malfunction
went unnoticed
by the FCC.

*The owner's manual
for your
'31 Bugatti Royale
is only available
in Italian.*

Your contractor built the private screening room in your home directly under your private bowling alley.

It takes all day
to walk down
to get the mail.

YOUR VISA CARD HAS A PALTRY TEN-MILLION-DOLLAR LIMIT.

When you catch a cold, the Center for Disease Control shows up to treat you.

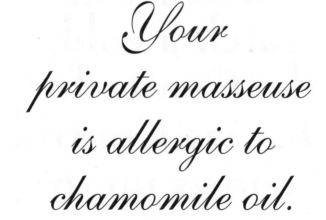

*Your
private masseuse
is allergic to
chamomile oil.*

You told your agent "nobody's interested in a movie about gay cowboys."

*The new bartender
at the Princeton Club
makes the martinis
with too much vermouth.*

A computer virus corrupted your e-closet database, so now you actually have to go in there and pick out your shoes by hand.

A sudden frost in the Netherlands delayed your daily shipment of fresh flowers for the dining room table.

Your die-hard fans
were disappointed to discover
that your latest album
played backwards
just sounds weird.

YOUR MANAGER,
AGENT, ACCOUNTANT, AND
EX-WIFE'S DIVORCE LAWYER
PLAY GOLF IN A REGULAR
FOURSOME AT THE RIVIERA.

Your ten-year-old daughter
has threatened to do
a tell-all interview with
Barbara Walters
unless you double
her trust fund.

David Crosby
was the best sperm donor
you could get
for your celebrity,
lesbian love child.

You can never remember which garage door opener goes with which Ferrari.

YOU JUST CAN'T FIND
A GOOD DOUBLE DECAF,
NONFAT SOY, FOAMLESS
LATTE, MOCHACCINO
WHEN YOU'RE ON LOCATION.

Your
Secret Service
code name
is Dumbass.

Your high society get-together with three hundred of your closest friends came to an abrupt end when Conrad Hilton found a towel with his last name on it in your guest bathroom.

There aren't any parking spaces large enough for your limousine at the 7-Eleven.

Your new co-anchor announced to the entire six o'clock news audience that she watched you every night when she was a little girl.

YOU SINGLE-HANDEDLY FINANCED
NATIONAL GEOGRAPHIC'S LATEST
EXPEDITION TO THE SOUTH POLE,
BUT THEY REFUSED TO BRING BACK
ANY MAGELLAN PENGUINS
TO LIVE ON THE ICE-SKATING RINK
IN YOUR BASEMENT.

Your star
on the Hollywood
Walk of Fame
is right next to
a popular
fire hydrant.

THE COMMERCIAL PROMOTING *CAUGHT ON CAMERA* FEATURES A CLIP FROM A SECURITY CAMERA SHOWING YOU MAKING A PURCHASE AT A SAN FRANCISCO PORN SHOP.

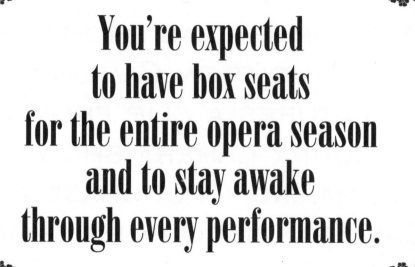

You're expected
to have box seats
for the entire opera season
and to stay awake
through every performance.

The tooth fairy auctioned your bicuspids for $3,000 on eBay.

DONALD TRUMP WON'T STOP ASKING YOU FOR A LOAN.

*No matter what gift
you receive for Christmas,
you've already got
three of them.*

EVERY TIME YOU TRY TO
GO FOR A SWIM
IN THE GROTTO POOL,
CHACHI IS IN THERE
DOING IT WITH THE
PLAYMATE OF THE MONTH.

The IRS has a
local task force
named after you.

Determined to own the best, you're forced to replace your computer every ten days.

When you fill out warranty registration forms, there's no box to check that comes remotely close to your income.

Surgeons used the
excess neck flesh
from your last facelift
to treat thirteen burn victims.
Three plan to sue.

Jessica Simpson kicked your ass on *Celebrity Jeopardy.*

To avoid being recognized whenever you go out in public, you have to wear a radiation suit.

THE BUFF POOL GUY
YOU HIRED TO KEEP
YOU COMPANY
WHILE YOUR HUSBAND
IS OUT OF TOWN
TURNED OUT TO BE GAY.

Mann's Chinese Theater
paved over your footprints
to make room for
Pauly Shore's.

You can't get CNN on your hand-held video baby monitor.

Your thirty-seat, state-of-the-art home theater now has authentic sticky floors —thanks to Roger Ebert and a mishap with a 64-ounce Big Gulp.

You were forced to divest your holdings after the SEC ruled you can own no more than half of all creation.

The DVD-player in
your Jaguar holds
only five DVDs
at a time.

It takes fifteen minutes for your hot tub to heat up to the right temperature.

You bought
a luxurious house
on Maui for your parents,
but now they expect you
to pay for the
domestic help.

New FAA regulations
require that
breast implants
be screened by
bomb-sniffing dogs.

You received
your $230-million
end-of-the-year bonus
in company stock—
not in cash as you
were led to believe.

Your favorite rib joint shut down in Chicago, so now you don't know from where you can have decent barbecue flown in.

You averaged twenty yards
a carry in your rookie season
and scored seventeen touchdowns,
but now you can't do an
end-zone dance to save your life.

Your adjusted gross income won't fit in the TurboTax box.

You missed
making *Forbes* magazine's list
of "World's Richest People"
by one.

You can't fit any more cars into your 24-car garage.

Your co-presenter at the Grammy Awards is Eminem.

Every time you
answer the phone
it's Woody Allen,
Roman Polanski, or
Jerry Seinfeld calling for
your teenage daughter.

YOUR ESTRANGED FATHER
APPEARED ON *JENNY JONES*
AND REVEALED THAT
HE ABANDONED YOU
BECAUSE YOU WET THE BED
UNTIL AGE SIXTEEN.

Whenever your name appears in a celebrity gossip column, it is always under the headline "Where are they now?"

Flying exclusively in your own private Learjet means you never rack up any frequent flier miles.

A mix-up with
a local subcontractor left you
with gold-plated toilets and
Italian marble fixtures in the
master bathroom.

You didn't realize that you accidentally left your skis at your château in Zermatt until you got to your château in Bariloche.

Your wife refuses to take golf lessons from anyone but Tiger Woods.

*There's no first class
on the express lifts
at Aspen.*

❄ ❄ ❄ ❄ ❄ ❄

Leonardo DiCaprio
puked in your limo
on the way home from
the *Titanic* premiere
and the carpet
still stinks in there.

You try to buy
your kids' love,
but they keep
raising the price
every year.

Groupies tell you,
"My mother made out
to your records."

Amway reps still think they can make you even richer.

You suspect that your daughter is sleeping with your body guard.

When they said,
"Steven and Julia
loved your screenplay,"
they were talking about
Steven Seagal and
Julia Louis-Dreyfus,
not Steven Spielberg
and Julia Roberts.

PAPARAZZI RESPECT YOUR PRIVACY.

As an honorary board member of the Sierra Club, you can no longer wear your sable coat.

You can't find
an ottoman
to match your
Louis XIV chair.

Your claymation
namesake on
Celebrity Death Match
looks like
Ozzie Osbourne.

Who's Who in America misspelled your middle name, prompting *Dun & Bradstreet* to do the same.

You can't believe that "I have more money than God" does not automatically exempt you from jury duty.

The photographer at the
Division of Motor Vehicles
snapped an extra picture
that wound up in
The National Enquirer.

An air traffic controller made you move your plane off the LAX runway before your stylist finished the third rinse and blow dry.

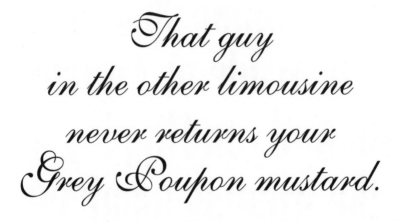

That guy
in the other limousine
never returns your
Grey Poupon mustard.

A cameo shot at the Academy Awards showed you flipping off the winning nominee.

Zero-percent financing
is of absolutely
no interest to you.

Your sister sold your
cell phone number
to obsessed fans
to make some
quick cash.

Your wine steward chilled a bottle of your Rothchild '57 one degree too cold, devastating its true flavor.

The air freshener they use at the Plaza Hotel makes you break out in hives.

A tropical rainstorm
in Key West
shorted out
the fax machine
on your Jet Ski.

It took two years
and seven of the world's
most renowned allergists
to determine that your
sinus condition is a reaction
to your Hungarian
goose-down pillow.

Your neighbors refused to permit construction of the third great pyramid on your estate.

You're suffering from a severe case of tennis elbow.

The recommended price range for your office party gift exchange is in the low five figures.

When you
made a guest appearance
on the celebrity version of
Who Wants to be a Millionaire?,
you flubbed the $500 question and
your favorite charity
ended up with the
home version of the game
and a case of aerosol cheese.

The President of the United States only comes to see you when he needs money.

YOU HAD TO BUILD
AN ANNEX ONTO YOUR HOME
TO STORE ALL THE GIFTS
YOU'VE RECEIVED FROM
FOREIGN HEADS OF STATE.

Your fans expect you
to wear all those
ridiculous outfits from the
Paris fashion shows.

YOUR SECOND HOME
IN PALM SPRINGS OVERLOOKS
THE FIFTEENTH HOLE OF
A CHAMPIONSHIP GOLF COURSE,
AND MORE THAN ONCE
A WAYWARD GOLFBALL
HAS COME FLYING THROUGH THE
GLASS DOOR OF YOUR STEAM BATH.

You had to bail on
Conan O'Brien
because they forgot
to remove the
blue M&M's from the
Green Room again.

After you paid $900
for a pair of front row tickets
to see *The Producers*,
Rip Torn stood in for
an ailing Nathan Lane.

You're expected to understand obscure Latin phrases, intelligently discuss the World Bank, and enjoy playing Scrabble.

You can't remember if the former pool boy is your fifth or sixth husband.

You think
food stamps are
edible postage.

You can't figure out
how to program your
robotic dog
to stop humping
your leg.

Your high-definition,
state-of-the-art,
65-inch, flat-screen television
receives 50,000 channels,
but 49,999 of them
seem to broadcast
Korean infomercials
around the clock.

THE LLADROS
THAT YOU KEEP RECEIVING
FROM AUNT SADIE
AND STORE IN THE ATTIC
KEEP ESCALATING IN VALUE.

The new album
your former bandmates
recorded with a new
look-alike frontman
outsold all your
previous releases
combined.

Maury Povitch
had the gall to ask you
not tell the same anecdote that
you told on Letterman,
Leno, and Oprah.

An audit of
Heidi Fleiss's books
revealed that you are
personally responsible
for twenty percent
of her revenues.

You're still depressed about losing to Richard Gere as *People*'s "Sexiest Man Alive."

THE NATIONAL ENQUIRER
SPREAD A VICIOUS RUMOR
THAT YOU ARE ACTUALLY
STRAIGHT.

The Stage Deli named
a new sandwich after you,
but its ingredients are
Cheez Whiz and
Marshmallow Fluff
on Wonder Bread.

You had to spend a week
searching all sixty rooms
of your Beverly Hills home
for your hand carved,
ebony croquet mallet.

You love your subscription,
front-row box seats
at the Hollywood Bowl,
but you find the wine selection
appallingly lackluster.

When your wife was arrested
for shoplifting in Beverly Hills,
she told the police that
she did it for excitement—
because you haven't been able
to perform sexually for years.

Every December
you must hire
a small company
to address and sign
your 20,000 holiday
greeting cards.

Your Q rating
has shrunk so small
that you have no choice
but to go on *Larry King Live*
and reveal that as a child
you were abducted by aliens who
sexually abused your karma.

Your manager keeps urging you to stand next to Jennifer Lopez to make your booty look smaller.

👑

The closest Wal-Mart
is two townships away.

The years you spent performing Shakespeare in summer stock did not adequately prepare you for your breakout role in *Dude, Where's My Car?*

You've had the
ice crusher in
your stretch limo
replaced three times,
but it's still
on the fritz.

HOWARD STERN CALLS YOUR MOTHER MORE OFTEN THAN YOU DO.

Angelina Jolie
is co-starring
in a movie
with your husband.

The Swiss ambassador to Cuba, who supplied you with your cigars, has been transferred to Nepal.

Hookers charge you full retail.

After fifteen years and seven Academy Awards, you're still not sure how to pronounce Cannes.

You need
173 iPods
to hold your
music collection.

YOUR LAST RAP CD
WAS TOO TAME
TO WARRANT A
PRMC WARNING STICKER.

Your next-door neighbor wants to tear down your 20,000-square-foot mansion to make room for his 40,000-square-foot servant's quarters.

Your starring role on
a popular television sitcom
was abruptly recast
and people now call you
"the first Darrin."

20/20 aired a segment showing how your celebrity diet can lead to apallingly bad acting and a possible appearance in a hideous infomercial.

YOUR BEST FRIENDS ARE YOUR BODY GUARDS.

YOUR $800-PER-HOUR LAWYER
JUST INFORMED YOU THAT
THERE'S NOTHING YOU CAN DO TO
PREVENT THE HIDDEN-CAMERA VIDEO
OF YOUR LAST BIKINI WAX
FROM CIRCULATING
AROUND THE INTERNET.

You're terrified by
the possibility that
there's more to life than
shopping, going out to lunch,
and having your nails done.

A neighbor called the police
when the Rolling Stones,
The Who, and Led Zeppelin
played in your backyard
for your 50th birthday bash.

YOU PAID FULL FARE
FOR YOUR SHIH TZU TO HAVE
HIS OWN FIRST-CLASS CABIN
ON THE *QUEEN MARY 2*,
BUT YOU STILL HAVE TO PROVIDE
YOUR OWN RAWHIDE CHEW STICK.

*You forgot to thank God
at the Golden Globe Awards,
so now He won't
return your calls.*

The Mediterranean salt air
wreaks havoc on
the fourteenth-century
Italian Renaissance tapestries
in your villa on the island of Capri.

When you flew
first class aboard
the Concorde to Paris,
the hot washcloths
handed out by
the flight attendants
were tepid.

Victoria's Secret
asked you to be the spokesperson
for their new line of
"Big and Beautiful"
lingerie.

THE TILE ON
THE BATHROOM FLOOR
OF YOUR GUEST HOUSE AT
THE KENNEDY COMPOUND
IN HYANNISPORT
WASN'T CAULKED PROPERLY
AROUND THE BASE OF THE SINK.

Your son insists upon living in the dormitory with everyone else at Oxford, but the three Secret Service agents living in the room next door hinder his social life.

WHEN YOU WENT FOX HUNTING
WITH THE ROYAL FAMILY,
PRINCE WILLIAM ACCIDENTALLY
SHOT A HOLE THROUGH
YOUR TOP HAT.

You can't decide whether
to spend the next three weeks
going on safari in Tanzania,
hiking Mount Everest,
or having a tummy tuck.

You don't have
a clue what the
Alternative Minimum Tax is,
but you end up paying it
every year.

When you're onstage,
women throw
their underwear at you—
mostly Extra Large
with Super Control Top.

*Your Aussie accent
was so thick, they hired
Arnold Schwarzenegger
to dub your lines.*

YOU ACCIDENTALLY WORE YOUR CUMMERBUND UPSIDE DOWN THIRTY YEARS AGO AT SWIFTY'S OSCAR PARTY AND NOW E! SHOWS THE CLIP EVERY MARCH.

You had no idea that the three bathrooms aboard the four-masted schooner you had custom-built in France would include bidets.

You've been repeatedly asked to install TiVo in your servants' quarters.

The mechanic you have on salary
to maintain your high-speed,
triple loop-de-loop roller coaster
seems to be making off with
a few too many crates of WD-40.

Just because you
hired a plane to skywrite your
marriage proposal over Monte Carlo,
your wife expects you to remember
your wedding anniversary every year.

You're willing to pay
$40 million to the Russians
to take you up to the
International Space Station,
but they refuse to provide you
with French space food.

The pyrotechnics firm you hired to produce fireworks for your daughter's wedding accidently blew up your gazebo.

Anyone who ever attended your high school wants to be your insurance agent.

WHEN YOU ASKED
LLOYD'S OF LONDON
TO INSURE YOUR LEGS
FOR ONE MILLION DOLLARS
AS A PUBLICITY STUNT,
THEY TOLD YOU
TO SAVE YOUR MONEY.

President Bill Clinton keeps begging you to get him into your golf club.

The new administration
rejected your request
to be appointed head of
the Treasury department
because you already have
most of the money anyway.

YOU USED YOUR
PARENTS' POLITICAL CONNECTIONS
TO GET ELECTED GOVERNOR,
BUT SOMEHOW YOUR
DOPEY, YOUNGER BROTHER
USED THOSE SAME CONNECTIONS
TO GET ELECTED PRESIDENT.

The co-op board denied your application to buy a $12-million co-op because they didn't like the final episode of your top-rated sitcom.

The McDonald's in your mansion still makes the coffee too hot.

When President Jimmy Carter
asks you to build a house
for Habitat for Humanity,
he expects your crew to construct
a 21-story apartment complex
with a pool and spa.

Your personal trainer has a personal trainer.

When you were arrested for picking up a transvestite prostitute on Sunset Boulevard, no one believed you were simply giving a damsel in distress a lift.

Your agent told you to lose twenty pounds before you audition for the lead role in *The John Candy Story.*

Your name appears
in the movie credits
two points smaller
than the FBI warning
not to copy the film.

You had to hire
a former U.S. Secretary of State
to read the daily *Wall Street Journal,*
New York Times, London Times,
Washington Post, Boston Globe, and
Los Angeles Times for you.

You changed your name to
an unpronounceable symbol
as a publicity stunt,
and now it's impossible to
make dinner reservations.

THE CONSULTANT YOU HIRED TO COME UP WITH A UNIQUE NAME FOR YOUR CHILD WAS SHOCKED TO LEARN THAT MOON UNIT AND DWEEZIL WERE ALREADY TAKEN.

Your celebrity golf charity paired you up with O.J. Simpson.

*You're not sure
if you caught your
venereal disease from
Madonna, Tonya Harding,
or Dennis Rodman.*

Your manicurist refused to rearrange her vacation to Hawaii around your standing pedicure appointment.

None of the casinos in Las Vegas have a high enough maximum to make any of the games interesting.

Blockbuster features your latest exercise video in the horror section.

The fat from your ass
that was injected
into your lips
is developing cellulite.

You'd think people could remember who the *second* man to walk on the moon was, but *nooooooooooo*.

The best address you could get was Beverly Hills 90209.

All of your
NBA teammates
have way more
out-of-wedlock children
than you do.

YOUR PLATINUM-SELLING GIRL GROUP BROKE UP WHEN YOU REFUSED TO GRANT POWER-OF-ATTORNEY TO THE LEAD SINGER'S FATHER.

*Your stalkers
have their own website
where they share tips
on how to break into your estate
and steal your dirty laundry.*

The Library of Congress keeps borrowing books from your personal library.

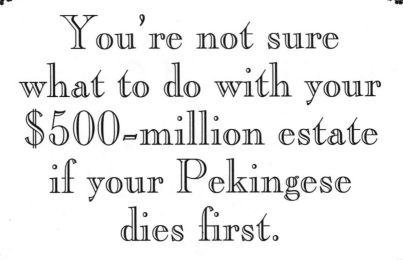

You're not sure
what to do with your
$500-million estate
if your Pekingese
dies first.

*Just before
your turn to speak,
the leader of the free world
puked in your lap.*

The Metropolitan Museum of Modern Art won't stop pestering you to loan them your Van Gogh collection.

The IRS refused
to let you write off
$50,000 for prostitution services,
even though it was obviously
research for your next movie.

A mix-up at the dry cleaners forced you to wear an Armani garment bag to the Fashion Awards.

The Park Avenue
condo board kicked you out
just because your matching
Persian Lions
ate the cleaning service.

The last time you played polo, you threw out your pinkie.

YOUR SUPERMODEL GIRLFRIEND DUMPED YOU FOR CLAY AIKEN.

Out of all the flight attendants
you could have taken back
to your hotel room,
you chose the one
who was wired.

Owning 3,876 pairs of shoes forced you to hire a full-time shoe maintenance crew.

WHEN YOU RENTED
AN ELEPHANT FOR YOUR
FOUR-YEAR-OLD DAUGHTER'S
BACKYARD BIRTHDAY PARTY,
IT DRANK ALL THE CHAMPAGNE
FROM YOUR HOT TUB.

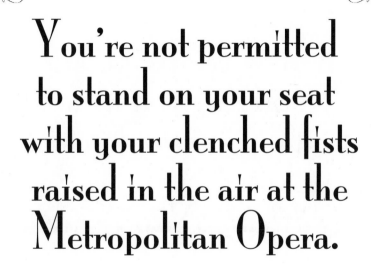

You're not permitted
to stand on your seat
with your clenched fists
raised in the air at the
Metropolitan Opera.

Your new television sitcom, starring you as a fictional version of yourself, was killed in the ratings by *Flying Nun* reruns.

The $100,000 donation
you made to your favorite charity
was overshadowed by the
$100-million donation
made by Bill Gates
later that same day.

Kids are finding
hidden messages in your music
instructing them to study,
get good grades, and
make something of themselves.

Destiny's Child
refused to perform at your
birthday party because
"it's too creepy with just
one guy sitting there."

Your publicist
insists the only way
you'll get any press
is by becoming
a Scientologist
and marrying
Lisa Marie Presley.

Your cell phone is so small you've already lost three of them in your purse.

The two pandas in your private zoo refuse to mate in captivity.

Liposuction turned "innie" into an "outie."

Even the French think your movies suck.

HUMOR

You can't fit any more cars into your 24-car garage.

Wish you were rich and famous? Think again. Life on easy street can be terribly bumpy.
You may wish you had the problems that accompany fame and fortune, until you discover
the rich have more of everything, including more things to complain about. *It takes the
Pizza Hut delivery guy thirty minutes just to get from the front gate of your property to your
front door. When the Houston Astros play the Baltimore Orioles, you're not sure which team to
root for because you own them both. Your seat on the New York Stock Exchange doesn't vibrate.
The President of the United States only comes to see you when
he needs money.* This hysterical collection of self-absorbed
grumbles from the lap of luxury makes the perfect gift for
the person who doesn't realize he has everything.

$8.95 U.S.
$12.95 Canada
Distributed by
Independent Publishers Group

JOEY GREEN is the author of 36 books, including *The Jolly
President (or Letters George W. Bush Never Read)* and *Polish
Your Furniture with Panty Hose*. DEBBIE GREEN is a former
television commercial producer. ALAN CORCORAN is the
coauthor of *Senior Moments* and *You Know You've Reached
Middle Age If* . . . They all live in Southern California.

ISBN 0-9772590-0-5

9 780977 259007

50895

Printed in India